I0510271

Purpose,

~~not~~ Perfect.

Jacqueline Thorne

Table of Contents

Introduction

You have within you a perfect purpose, but it doesn't come from you being perfect, it simply is perfectly who you always were. You have a purpose in life. You are meant for great things. When we allow ourselves to remove ourselves from the demand of perfection and understand that everything we need is already in us, that we will make mistakes but that even the times that we fall are just us learning and growing and moving on to that purpose that we have in life. Today is your day to embrace that you have a purpose, and it does not come from you being perfect.

The Joy Of Living In My Purpose

As I write this book, I find myself in joy thinking about where I am now versus where I was. Looking around at all the amazing opportunities that happened in my life, that I am able to help people live empowered, equipped with the discipline to identify the goals that they have in life and then go beyond seeing them to accomplishing them. For each person that I work with it's different, but it's so exciting to see it come through. In my day to day work life, I've been blessed with a lot of accomplishments. Now I can look around and see the projects, grants and policies that I manage, are the result of me saying yes.

I create strategies for huge design projects, work with professionals, and really make a difference. Not just for myself, but in the city and communities that I work in.

I've had several awards for closing a huge grant for an infrastructure called the B&P Tunnel. It's over 140 years old. It sat on the shelf, not being worked on for several years. I was granted the opportunity to step in, complete the project from cradle to grave on time and under budget, which returned several million dollars back to the government. It was the biggest project for the state agency as well as the state of Maryland in terms of value, at that time. Completing that project was an amazing accomplishment, in addition, I was awarded Employee Of The Year and a Quality Initiative award. It was a huge infrastructure project, and honestly, if you had asked me when I was twenty, I probably wouldn't have believed it was possible. But now here I am making decisions, managing things, building powerful relationships as I live as a strong, independent woman. I am a homeowner, I own my own home & vehicle I live a good life filled with laughter, family and friends. My life is full and I found myself being asked, How did you accomplish that? I also asked myself, what's next, what do I do with all of this great information? The answer was document, share and inspire. And now, I don't run from my greatness, I use this to help others be encouraged. If they can learn to believe in themselves. If they learn & begin to document their achievements, they too have a purpose and that that purpose will be fulfilled in their life as they do all that they're meant to do.

As a leader and subject matter expert, I am responsible for all aspects of the project. I am where the buck starts and ends. This is not an easy experience. It is most certainly not impossible, however for many to attempt and furthermore accomplish is a rarity. One of my colleagues once characterized my projects as insane to manage. I could elaborate in granular detail however, I want you to understand the vast umbrella of responsibility. It is my calling, my assignment and I said yes, I will accept and manage these projects.

Embracing God's Gifts In Me

You have to understand, it wasn't always this way. I'm an only child and at ten years old, my father, who had been in the military, divorced my mother and turned to drugs. From age ten to twenty-four, my dad was far from a positive role model in my life. My mom worked hard. She is an amazing single mom. who praised & gave all that she could, but sometimes what I really longed for was my dad. I was afraid that everybody that saw me didn't see who I was. In my thoughts I believed people looked at me but rather than seeing me they just saw my father, or a representation or reminder of him. This caused me to be shy, lacking confidence as a young lady. I thought maybe even the divorce, maybe even my father turning to drugs was somehow my fault. Sometimes what I really just needed was my father to show me what a man's love feels like, to tell me I was beautiful and that he loved me. Because I didn't have this, what it left me with was a lack of confidence, a sense that I wasn't good enough, that I wasn't worthy and a strong belief that people saw me just as they saw my dad. I got attention throughout school by being smart, accomplishing things academically, but in my head, there was that same message, "I was a drug addict's daughter." I made lots of mistakes as we all do. Looking for a dad in the relationships that I had. I even found myself in a long term bad relationship with a man who had a different kind of addiction but was still every bit of an addict. I made these mistakes because I was looking for that love that I didn't have in my life. I always had the faith that I'd grown up in my life. I had always journalcd, poured out my emotions in writing in a very cathartic manner. But what I had to learn was how to begin to believe. To believe what I was writing. To believe that the beliefs that I had were real. I had to be the one to embrace the gifts that God gave me, to take the support from my family and friends to take on the task of my purpose.

I was the one that had to believe, no one else could do it for me. But as I began to see myself differently, to believe in myself and to see that I did have a purpose, things began to get better. It didn't happen overnight, it was a process. But I can look back now, and I can see through all of those things that I've been through that I have a purpose. That I have been growing from where I was to who I am. You have a purpose, and it's not being perfect. You are brighter right now than you assume that you are. If you're like me, I tried to be perfect to somehow erase the scars I felt in life. I thought that if I just could only accomplish perfection that then people would see me differently, that it would somehow erase the stain of the disease that my father had. But as we begin to see that our purpose doesn't come from our perfection but rather simply you were created perfectly for your purpose as we are. As we grow to believe in that, your purpose, then it can come to the light. Ask yourself, "Who am I? What are the goals that I have in life? What do I want to be? What do I want to do with my life?" And then realize that you already have a purpose, that purpose has always been there. You were born with unique gifts & talents to fulfill purpose. It's never had anything to do with you being perfect.

Becoming The Diamond You Are

Knowing that your purpose does not come through your perfection, how does that feel? Does that make you feel released? I want you to understand that now is your time to try. To stop restricting yourself, but simply move forward. You see, trying is succeeding. As we try things, sometimes we accomplish what we try, and sometimes we fail. But we get back up, and we try again, and we get better. You see, it's not where we start but where we're going. It's about the little accomplishments that we're making and along the way we begin to learn that as we believe in ourselves, we can reach our purpose. We can surrender to the process and understand that we are a diamond. But just like finding a diamond, you're going to have to dig for it. You're going to have to dig through lots of coal, setting aside a bunch of rocks, through dirt and sediment to find those diamonds that are in there. A sifting has to take place to identify the authenticity of a diamond. Diamonds need to be certified by a jeweler, however, only a diamond can cut a diamond. You can see into a diamond but not through a diamond.

You have to go through this process, but on the other end, what you will achieve is that heart goal that you have inside. There is a beauty a sparkle and radiant light inside of you. And then, from that goal, you can create another goal, and that then becomes a new beginning. There are so many facets to you, sometimes we can't see past the current goal that we have that we'd like to accomplish, but what I want you to understand is that you are going to accomplish this goal and then I want you to be ready for the next. Your accomplishments become the examples of the successes you had. They become the fuel for you knowing that you're going to get to your next thing. You see, as we accomplish even the little things, we find a knowing. We know that it can be done.

The Support You Have All Around You

I had to learn how to vent without being emotional. I had to learn how to find support. When I began to actually accept the support, I began to see that I had a mom and aunties and cousins, mentors, even friends who were there to support me. But we have to be willing to take the support. First, we have to see that we need it, then we have to accept it and then learn to lean on those that will support you. There are people in your life right now, I'm sure, that are wanting to support you, and others in your community that if you reach out to, absolutely will. Especially if you are a leader, the go to person. You find yourself the leader in everything, pushing forward all on your own because you don't feel like you have the support. Doing it all on your own takes so much time, energy and your purpose needs you ready to perform well. As a recovering perfectionist, I know you may want perfection. Sometimes, completing the task is the perfection even if it is not the way you planned it, it's done. When we learn to lean on others, to reach out to other people, we can begin to accomplish what we're going for and reach our purpose even quicker.

As you grow in a leadership, you need to learn how to share the light with other people. As a leader, you're responsible for a lot of things. Sometimes you have a vast umbrella of responsibilities. You're working on a project that you put time, effort and energy into and then you have to sit back and watch somebody else representing the thing that you know inside and out, but that's not what your purpose is in that minute. Rather it's to sit back and watch them glow. Your glow is not dimmed by their accomplishments. And as a leader, what you find is, learning how to help others in your life shine is one of the greatest accomplishments you'll ever have. You elevate when you help build another leader.

What Is Your Purpose?

My purpose is to bring order to chaos. Bring a balance to what's falling apart. To get you out of comfort zones. My business is to get personal with people. Establish trust and communication to multiple parties. The ability to see the entire picture through to the end. Your purpose is to first start where you are and be curious enough to be a sponge and absorb all you can on the subjects that you can't stop thinking about. What has you up late at night thinking about it or do you dream about something so great it brings joy when you recall the memory of it. Speak your dreams, write down or share them with people you trust and love you and support you. Bring life to your purpose by naming it, you can change it later or it may evolve into something else. I know what it feels like to operate in purpose, for a purpose, on purpose. It is unpredictable at times tedious, and rewarding to see something through to fruition.

When you treat a lion like a cat they become domesticated. You are the Lion/Lioness, you just needed a reminder of how powerful and capable your are. The lion has sharp senses, quick responses, and is royalty. That is who you are, powerful, capable, leading with your sharp discernment and you most certainly are royal. Are you forgetting that you are gifted and outstanding? You are wonderfully made. I want to remind you of who you are.

One of the ways you overlook your purpose is thinking that an opportunity or situation doesn't look like what you developed in your mind. You've built the entire storyline in your thoughts. You painted the walls, colored shapes and sizes of the decor, wrote scripts for the other people in your imagined version of what perfection looks like for you. If this sounds familiar or similar, you are attempting to be the Director of your own story. You're also producing and acting in a fantasized version of your life. There is a difference between fantasy and dreaming. Perfection is fantasy. Purpose is not predictable, it can be messy, chaotic, and unappealing.

Please don't stop dreaming, I want you to dream and aspire to be the best at what you are gifted to do. However, the fantasy developed in your head is PERFECT! I know about building unrealistic expectations and being totally devastated when nothing about my picture was perfect. I went through several cycles of chasing perfection throughout. I have the perfectionism disease. Perfectionism is my addiction. Addictions are hereditary, mine is being perfect. I am the research for this subject. I know this topic intimately. This is why I am passionate about living toward purpose. I hurt my own feelings developing these scenarios and being so crushed when they did not materialize. Living your dreams is not a straight road. Sometimes life is messy. There are detours and setbacks, but purpose is at the finish line.

Heading Towards Your Purpose

Wherever you are on your journey in life, I can tell you confidently that one day you will be a leader, or if your already a leader level up, be an intentional leader. But even now you need to understand, you need to begin to start learning from the background. Learning what it takes to be an effective leader by observing the examples of the good leaders that are in your life now. You have to also see that sometimes it's not always fun to be the leader. Leadership is a responsibility requiring sacrifice. When you are a leader, you have to be prepared to respond to opposition, failures, and complaints, put out the fires. The pressures of managing are often unpredictable.

You have to learn how to be able to take the heat along with the accolades. To learn how to shine the light on other people to celebrate their wins. To be a light in other people's lives. Leaders, build and nurture leaders. We never really know what our simple celebration of somebody else, our encouragement of them may do for them. My mom was so good at being encouraging, I learned compassion from her. In the end, we discover that people follow people that they like. You need to be the kind of person that people enjoy being around. Also, understand that this encouragement is something that not only helps them grow, but you never know when and where that person may come back into your life again. The impact of celebrating them will not only positively affect their life but in the future of yours. I experienced being in opposition on topic with business partners. Although we differed opinions, they liked & respected me. Whenever I see them, they are happy to see me and volunteer to be of assistance with any requests because they like me.

Often just like you, I've said to myself, "But I don't have the confidence." "You don't understand." "I'm young." "I don't have any money." "My mom's a single parent." "I just got into this new relationship with my boyfriend, and I really need to spend the time to make it work." "I don't really have more time to invest in something else because I already feel overcommitted." I learned the value of having your time. You have to make an effort to invest more time in yourself. Take money out of the scenario. There are always resources, grants, and other ways that you can get the money. Layaway or time released pay is ever increasing, an option for many goods & services. What you need to do is be disciplined. Do the things that you need to do for you to advance the life you want, to move towards the career that you want, the lifestyle you desire. The reality is, you do whatever it takes to get what you want. Utilize that same energy to achieve what you need to fulfill your purpose.

Rather than seeking validation from other people, remember that you're worthy, that you have a purpose and see how valuable you are in yourself. Then you can live the life that you've always dreamed of, rather that being travel or the career path that you have, you can succeed. Because you don't need to be perfect to reach your goal. Perfection doesn't help you get to your purpose, it is simply your purpose in this world. You don't need to be perfect, you just need to be in action, headed towards that goal, doing the powerful things that you can do to be able to reach that purpose.

Die to yourself, the you, you are right now. I do not mean this literally! The you that is comfortable with the way your life is right now. The you that knows what to expect and how to respond. You will need to stretch and evolve to elevate to a new stage in your life. Can you or will you die to your old self? What does this mean? To move forward and do something amazing with someone like a spouse, partnership, a project you must shed who you are now to grow into the new you in that relationship.

The Butterfly Effect

I like to use the Butterfly Effect as a visual resource. The beautiful butterflies you see in gardens, landscapes, and green spaces are the result of a metaphoric process. That Monarch, Peacock, Painted Lady or Red Admiral was a Caterpillar in its prior life. The process to get to the butterfly takes work. The work is in stages, but it is work that is gratifying. The butterfly has its own process. We did not see each step, but we get to see the beauty of the process, work & efforts. Purpose is like a Caterpillar becoming a Butterfly.

Apology Letter - To Anyone Who

Needs This

It's been far too long for you to operate in this condition. Someone, somebody something owes you an apology. You would feel so much better to know that your pain was acknowledged and that the wrong words, act or event that has you angry and fearful or maybe apprehensive is long overdue. You need a cleansing for you to move on. I am so sorry! I apologize, I am regretful, and I genuinely wish to acknowledge the pain I created for you. I am responsible for your pain. I hurt you, and you didn't deserve this. I left you and didn't prepare you for a life without me. I was hurting and did not know how to work through my emotions. I had not experienced joy or satisfaction or been celebrated. Because I knew what hurting & pain & doubt felt like, I imposed this pain on you. I didn't love myself, nor did I know how to love you. Please forgive me, you need to forgive me to free me and you. You don't need to be obligated to serve this pain, stop feeding and providing fuel for this pain to grow. You need to forgive me, so this anguish does not turn into a physical disease living in your body and taking over your mind and mental wellness. Forgive me, and you shall be forgiven. Love the unlovable, and you will be loved. Break the cycle, and it ends here. Forgive me and love yourself. Forgive me and lift the weight of that pain off your shoulders. Forgive me so you can be free.

Find A Mentor

Thirty years ago, when I was starting this journey for myself, we didn't have the resources and the internet and the things that we can do so easily for free to be able to research and find online courses to be able to advance who we are as a person. Opportunities to network, to meet other people, maybe even in free meet-up groups. An opportunity to reach out to someone that you admire in their career or personal path that you're following, follow them on social media and then reach out to them. Ask them questions like, "How can I get an internship to get into this field?" "What does it take to get into this business?" Additionally, take the time to volunteer your effort. Pour into somebody else that needs your help. What you'll find is when you help someone else, you're also helping yourself. All of these things help us strengthen our communication muscle, you're going to need to communicate with people and be a people person if you're going to do any type of work that's with the public. I even suggest finding somebody in the field that you're going towards and do mock interviews with them for the job that you want. Practice it. Practice so that you can know how to be able to say the things and be the person that someone looking for that job needs to have, be, and do. Again, it's not being perfect in the interview, it's simply learning from these things and growing.

Surrender To The Process

There is always a process ...A beginning a middle, a transition, mistakes, a beginning and an end, a success, a failure, a middle, a win, a loss. You get the picture. Plans don't often work the way you envisioned them. Countless times corporations, individuals, visionaries have failed and started over. When you realize there is a process and a learning curve, a test run you surrender to the process and learn from mistakes or miscalculations. Embrace your mistakes, they are your test lab for a greater version of yourself or what you are creating. Your knowledge in your capabilities are uniques and priceless. No one can emulate your special gifts and talents. Your gifts are a present from God. You will be challenged but you will succeed.

There will be some tough heartbreaks along your journey to your purpose. In certain instances it will be a person that you care deeply about, maybe you love them. It may feel like this is your eternal love but it's ok to recognize that this may not last and that if you really want love in your life, you have to love yourself first. Love makes you vulnerable for pain and pleasure. Loving yourself first is the most significant act you can do. This is self-care at its highest level. When you love and appreciate yourself, take care of yourself, be patient with yourself, treat yourself, have peace with yourself. All of this self-love will become the measure by which you can judge someone else's love for you. You will know what love feels like and your partners love will feel familiar. Your partner must also love themselves so that you both come whole to the relationship. Your happiness should not come from someone else. Your happiness should be enhanced by someone else. I pray this is making sense for you. It took me two decades to realize these lessons. I was not taught to love myself first. I grew up thinking I was supposed to love hard and give all that I could. I even made a vow to myself that the next relationship I was in, I was only 21 years old, I was going to love with all that I had without holding anything back so I would know that I tried it once. Despite all that I knew to be true and false, all the sunday school lessons, seeing my parents relationship implode and my Dad's absence in my life, I could not have met a more selfish and manipulative partner. Before it all ended some twenty years later, I knew the relationship was dead at least 10 years prior,

I kept on loving him until I had nothing to give. I want to be the vicarious lesson learned. I denied my purpose and moved around it, beside it and sometimes under it, I was stubborn and took a long route but I was graced the time I needed to heal and make my way back to my purpose. I did not get to skip steps because I waited so long to move in my purpose. I surrendered to the process and now I am capable of leaping into my talents.

Embrace Your Purpose

You are going to accomplish great things, and one of the things you need to learn to do is document your achievements. It's not going to happen all in one day, but as we continue from day to day and write down the things that we've accomplished, we will see great things. I like to make a list for myself of all the things that I want to do, not because I can get them done all in one day, but because I can do the things that I can do today and then handle more of the things on that list again tomorrow. As we look at this list, we can see and realize that we're accomplishing something, we're going towards that goal that we have in life. We can see all the things that we've accomplished. We can watch as we progress in life and we can celebrate the wins that we have as we fulfill our purpose. I also have began creating a lessoned learned documentation. Every event I facilitate or attend, I create a list of what worked, what failed or was missing and list solutions to improve that experience. I also discuss this with my fellow participants and the staff that assisted me. Becoming a good listener is imperative to your strength as a leader. Again remember, it's not about trying to be perfect, always succeeding and never failing, but just simply embracing the purpose that you have. Be unapologetic about your gifts. Own your word. Trust your instincts and go for it. Release being perfect and learn today to live in your purpose. The key to the success that you're going to have in life is purpose, not perfection.